The Household
Financial Record Book

The Household Financial Record Book

Create a user-friendly, hardcopy listing of your financial assets for your spouse and heirs.

T. Chris Clark

The Household Financial Record Book

November 2013

Cover Design: Chris Bailey Design

This book is dedicated to

Thomas C. Clark 1928 – 2006

*Devoted husband for over 50 years, loving father, Presbyterian Elder,
Korean War Veteran, Combat Medic and Bronze Star Recipient.
You, sir, are sorely missed.*

Table of Contents

ACKNOWLEDGMENTS

Many thanks to Rob Alexander for his review and creative ideas. Thanks also to Mike Clark for review and many good suggestions along the way. The excellent graphic design is due to Chris Bailey of *Chris Bailey Design*, and his help is also much appreciated. Last but not least, the editing skill of Nilla Childs of *Nilla Creates* was invaluable in producing this finished product.

INTRODUCTION

If your loved one were to die unexpectedly, would you know where to find his or her life insurance policy? What about the 401(k) plan that your spouse forgot to move/ roll over from Company X? Do you know whom to contact to access this account, or have the account number? Do you know where to find the will, military discharge papers, or stock certificates purchased decades ago? Do you know your spouse's online passwords? If you cannot answer these questions, this workbook may be the best investment you ever made.

There are far too many horror stories of months wasted attempting to identify and locate financial records and related assets after the death of a spouse, all of which could be avoided with some simple pre-planning. Without proper hardcopy documentation that is readily accessible, your accounts and other assets can easily be overlooked, and the information required to access your online accounts and online assets tends to evaporate in cyberspace.

Congratulations! You have taken the first step toward helping to provide for your loved ones in the event of your death. This workbook is intended to help you to list important financial accounts, critical passwords, and other personal assets and information in a simple and user-friendly manner, so as to simplify passing on these resources to those you care about most. The intent is to allow you to capture this important information, in a hard copy, so that resources will not be overlooked or lost.

Because of the sensitive nature of this information, store this document in a location that is not "visible" – preferably in a fire-proof safe or fire-proof file cabinet. Ensure that your spouse knows the lock combination, or location of the key. Generally do NOT store this information in your safe deposit box, as your heirs may not be able to access this location quickly in the event of your death.

OK, so let's get started. All you need to do is start recording information in the forms and tables that follow. In most cases, examples are provided. Some blank pages are provided at the end to allow customized listing of additional assets.

Disclaimer

This document is designed to facilitate listing of typical assets. While every effort has been made to be complete, it is not intended to be all-inclusive or comprehensive, and no warranty is made to that effect. Use of this document presupposes a level of trust in those who will receive the information recorded herein. Adequate means should be taken to safeguard this document. You, as the user, assume all such risks. You should abide by all applicable laws. All financial, tax and estate planning should be performed with the advice of competent professionals.

Personal Notes, Comments, and Directions
(This is NOT a Last Will and Testament)

_____
_____
_____
_____
_____
_____
_____
_____
_____
_____
_____
_____
_____
_____
_____
_____
_____
_____
_____
_____
_____
_____
_____
_____
_____
_____
_____
_____
_____
_____
_____
_____
_____
_____

Last Will and Testament

Location of Will: _____

Attorney Name: _____

Law Firm: _____

Attorney Phone: _____

Attorney Email: _____

Notes:
_____
_____
_____
_____
_____
_____
_____
_____
_____
_____
_____
_____
_____
_____
_____
_____
_____
_____
_____
_____
_____
_____
_____
_____
_____
_____
_____
_____
_____
_____
_____

Other Key Documents

Location of Marriage License: _____

Location of Social Security Card: _____

Location of Birth Certificate: _____

Location of Military Discharge Papers: _____

Location of Recent Tax Return(s): _____

Location of Power of Attorney Documents: _____

Location of Other Document: _____

Location of Other Document: _____

Location of Other Document: _____

Location of Other Document: _____

Notes: _____

_____

_____

_____

_____

_____

_____

_____

_____

_____

_____

_____

_____

_____

_____

_____

_____

_____

_____

_____

Life Insurance Policies

Company Name	Insured Name	Policy Number	Policy Amount $$	Beneficiary Name	Location of Policy	Insurance Agent Name	Insurance Agent Phone
Example:							
my insurance company	*Mark*	*123456*	*$400,000*	*Mary*	*Mary's safe deposit box at XYZ Bank*	*John Smith*	*(111) 555-3333*

Bank/Financial Accounts

Name of Bank	Type of Account	Account Number	Contact Name and Phone/Email	Website (For Online Accounts)	Approx. Amount $$	Login Username & Password	Location of Statements and Checkbooks
Example:							
XYZ Bank	*checking account*	*12345678*	*John Smith, (111) 555-1111*	*www.bankwebsite.com*	*~$5,000.*	*rsjones500 / mypassword*	*file cabinet, first drawer*

Retirement Accounts (401k, IRA, Roth IRA, 403b, etc.)

Type of Account	Name of Account/ Brokerage Firm	Account Number	Company/ Employer Name	Location of Documentation	Beneficiary Name	Approx. Amount $$	Notes (Describe *Required Minimum Distributions and Date*)
Example:							
401(k)	*financial firm name 401(k)*	*22222222*	*(my present/former employer that sponsored this plan)*	*top file drawer*	*Mary*	*$50,000.*	*(minimum distribution must be taken in February)*

Notes on Retirement Accounts

- Be sure to list accounts that still exist with previous employers!
- Ideally, rollover/consolidate accounts from previous employers.
- Provide username/password and web site information if the accounts are accessible online.
- Be sure that beneficiary information is up to date for each account.
- If minimum distributions are required, they should be listed, with the annual date due, to prevent incurring expensive penalties from the IRS.

Retirement Pension Plans with Current/Former Employers

Company	Account Number	Amount $$ per Month	Benefits Start Date	Contact Information	Contact Phone/Email	Location of Documentation	Notes
Example: *XYZ Company*	*222222*	*$500.*	*1/1/2020*	*XYZ Company Retirement Services, St. Louis, MO 11122*	*(111) 555-2222*	*fire safe, third drawer*	*This pension is applicable to surviving spouse.*

College Savings Plans (529 Plans)

State Hosting Plan	Participant Name	Beneficiary Name (Student's name)	Plan Website	Account Number	Approx. Amount $$	Contact Phone/Email	Notes: Username & Password
Example:							
VA	John Doe	Sally Doe	www.website.com	1234567	$10,000	(111) 555-3333	Jdoe / mypassword

College Savings Plans (Coverdell ESA)

Brokerage Hosting Account	Participant Name	Beneficiary Name (Student's name)	Plan Website	Account Number	Approx. Amount $$	Contact Phone/Email	Notes: Username & Password
Example:							
XYZ Financial	John Doe	Sally Doe	www.website.com	1234567	$10,000	(111) 555-3333	Jdoe / mypassword

UTMA Accounts (Uniform Transfers to Minors Act)

Brokerage/ Company	Participant (Custodian) Name	Beneficiary Name (Minor's name)	Plan Website	Account Number	Approx. Amount $$	Contact Phone/Email	Notes / Username & Password
Example:							
XYZ Financial	John Doe	Mark Doe	www.website.com	1234567	$15,000	(111) 555-3333	Jdoe / mypassword

Other Income Streams – Current and Future
(Annuities, Social Security, Veterans Benefits, Disability Benefits, etc)

Type of Benefit Income	Account Number	Amount $$ per Month	Benefits Start Date	Contact Information	Contact Phone/Email	Location of Documentation	Notes
Example: *annuity*	*222222*	*$500.*	*(ongoing)*	*XYZ Company 111 Any St. St. Louis, MO 22233*	*(111) 555-2222*	*fire safe, third drawer*	

Online Trading/Brokerage Accounts (Non-Retirement Accounts)

Brokerage Firm	Account Number	Website	Account Username and Password	Beneficiary Name	Approx. Value $$	Notes
Example:						
my broker	1111111	www.mybroker.com	MyUsername / (see notes)	Mary	$20,000.	password to this account is located --

Individual Stocks* – Purchased Directly from the Company
(Not Purchased through a Brokerage Account)

Company	Ticker Symbol	Account Number	Number of Shares	Approximate Value $$	Company Contact	Contact Phone/Email	Notes / Location of Paper Certificates / Documentation
Example: XYZ Company	ABC	1111111	100	$4500.	XYZ Investment Services	(333) 555-1212	fire safe, in folder for XYZ Co.

*Ideally, make sure your spouse's name is printed as a joint owner on paper stock certificates you own

US Savings Bonds*

Series	Denomination	Bond Serial Number	Issue Date	Maturity Date	Location	Notes
Example:						
EE Bonds	*$100.*	*12345678*	*5/30/2010*	*5/30/2015*	*fire safe in basement*	

*Ideally, make sure your spouse's name is printed as a joint owner on savings bonds you own

39

Real Estate

(Primary Home, Vacation Homes, Land, Rental Properties)

Property Street Address	Property City, State, Zip	Cost / Year of Purchase	Estimated Value, $$	Mortgage Company	Amount of Loan	Loan Number	Location of Title	Notes
Example:								
111 Any Street	Denver, CO 12345	2002	$150,000	XYZ Company	$100,000	12345678	fire safe	loan payment due monthly

Vehicles
(Automobiles, Boats, Airplanes, Motorcycles, RVs, Four-Wheelers, Jet-Skis, Tractors, etc.)

Vehicle Type	Year / Model	Description	Cost / Year of Purchase	Estimated Value, $$	Location of Title	Notes
Example:						
Buick	*2010 LeSabre*	*white, four door*	*2010*	*$8,000*	*fire safe, "cars" folder*	*registration in glove box of car*

43

Storage Lockers / Self-Storage

Name of Storage Company	Address	Locker Number	Contact Person/ Phone/Email	Contents of Locker	Location and Key ID OR Lock Combination

Safe Deposit Boxes

Bank Name	Address (*Safe Deposit Box Location*)	Box Number	Contact Person / Bank Phone	Contents of Box*	Location and Key ID or Lock Combination

*Safe Deposit boxes should NOT be used to store information or items needed immediately in the event of your death, as your heirs may not have immediate access to them.

Antiques / Collectibles (Table 1 of 3)

Type	Description	Estimated Value, $$	Cost Basis, $$	Year Acquired	Location of Documentation / Appraisal	Notes
Example:						
antique desk	*large oak desk, 6 drawers, vintage 1900*	*$1500*	*$1000*	*1995*	*safe deposit box at XYZ bank*	

Antiques / Collectibles (Table 2 of 3)

Type	Description	Estimated Value, $$	Cost Basis, $$	Year Acquired	Location of Documentation / Appraisal	Notes
Example:						
antique desk	*large oak desk, 6 drawers, vintage 1900*	*$1500*	*$1000*	*1995*	*safe deposit box at XYZ bank*	

Antiques / Collectibles (Table 3 of 3)

Type	Description	Estimated Value, $$	Cost Basis, $$	Year Acquired	Location of Documentation / Appraisal	Notes
Example:						
antique desk	*large oak desk, 6 drawers, vintage 1900*	*$1500*	*$1000*	*1995*	*safe deposit box at XYZ bank*	

Miscellaneous Assets (Table 1 of 2)

Type	Description	Estimated Value, $$	Cost Basis, $$	Year Acquired	Location of Documentation / Appraisal	Notes
Example:						
stereo	*Kenwood*	*$800.*	*$800*	*2012*	*file cabinet, second drawer*	

55

Miscellaneous Assets (Table 2 of 2)

Type	Description	Estimated Value, $$	Cost Basis, $$	Year Acquired	Location of Documentation / Appraisal	Notes
Example:						
stereo	*Kenwood*	*$800.*	*$800*	*2012*	*file cabinet, second drawer*	

Firearms (Table 1 of 2)

Make / Model	Description, Caliber or Gauge	Estimated Value, $$	Cost Basis, $$	Year Acquired	Location of Documentation / Appraisal	Storage Location of Firearm
Example:						
Winchester Model 70 bolt action	*30-06*	*$800*	*$600*	*1995*	*safe deposit box at XYZ bank*	*gun safe in basement.*

Firearms (Table 2 of 2)

Make / Model	Description, Caliber or Gauge	Estimated Value, $$	Cost Basis, $$	Year Acquired	Location of Documentation / Appraisal	Storage Location of Firearm
Example: *Winchester Model 70 bolt action*	*30-06*	*$800*	*$600*	*1995*	*safe deposit box at XYZ bank*	*gun safe in basement.*

Heirlooms

Item / Description	Location of Item	Location of Appraisal	Significance of Item ("The Story Behind It") OR Location of More Extensive Description	Estimated Value
Example: *gold tie tack*	*safe deposit box at XYZ bank*	*top file drawer, file "Heirlooms"*	*Tie tack was inherited from Grandpa Jones, who obtained it in North Africa during WWII.*	*~$500.*

Recurring Bills (Loan Payments, Utilities, Health/Life Insurance, etc.)
(See Separate List for "Recurring Bills Paid by Automatic Withdrawal")

Company	Type of Bill	Account Number	Approximate Amount $$	Company Address	Company Contact	Contact Phone	Notes / Location of Documentation

Recurring Bills Paid by Automatic Withdrawal
(Loan Payments, Utilities, Health/Life Insurance, etc.)

Company	Type of Bill	Bank Drafted	Bank Account Number	Approx. Billing Amount $$	Company Address/Website	Contact Name/ Phone/ Email	Notes / Location of Documentation / Login Information

Credit Card Accounts

Card Type	Financial Institution	Account Number	Website	Phone Number	Location of Documentation	Login Username / Password
Example:						
Mastercard	*XYZ bank*	*1111-2222-3333-4444*	*www.mybank.com*	*(111) 555-2222*	*file cabinet, third drawer*	*Jdoe / mypassword*

Email Accounts

E-mail Address	Website	Username	Password	Are Recurring Bills Sent to This Address?	Notes (Describe Primary Use of Account, Including Recurring Bills that are Sent to Account)
Example:					
Jdoe@gmail.com	*www.gmail.com*	*MyUsername*	*MyPassword*	*yes*	*Utility bills are sent to this email address.*

Fire Safes and Gun Safes Located at Home

Type of Safe	Location	Lock Combination OR Location / Description of Key(s)	Contents of Safe	Notes
Example:				
fire safe	*basement*	*keys in top dresser drawer, key number E110*	*life insurance policies, coin collection*	.

My Financial Professionals

(Key Investment Advisors, Insurance Agents, Attorneys, Tax Preparers, Estate Planners)

Name of Professional	Occupation	Company Name / Location	Contact Phone/ Email	Service Provided / Notes
Example:				
John Doe	*life insurance agent*	*XYZ Life Insurance Co. Atlanta, GA*	*(111) 555-3333 / email address*	*life insurance policy, disability insurance policy.*

Miscellaneous 1: _____

Miscellaneous 2: _____

Miscellaneous 3: _____

Miscellaneous 4: _____

Miscellaneous 5: _____

CPSIA information can be obtained at www.ICGtesting.com
Printed in the USA
BVOW04s1919010316

438635BV00020B/137/P

9 780615 915302